Just Tasting

Volume 2

More Quick and Easy
Mini Appetizers, Soups & Salads
Recipes for Casual Entertaining

by Robert Zollweg

Written and Designed by Robert Zollweg
Photography by Rick Luettke, www.luettkestudio.com
Graphics by Gary Raschke and Robert Zollweg
Art Direction Gary Raschke

Library of Congress Cataloging-in-Publication Data:

Just Tasting Volume Two
More Mini Appetizers, Soups and Salad Recipes
for Casual Entertaining by Robert Zollweg

ISBN 978-0-615-67332-5

Printed in the United States of America
R.R. Donnelley and Company

I'd like to dedicate this cookbook to

Art, Nancy, Michael and Nicole

There are so many people to thank for making this cookbook a reality.

First and foremost, Steve and Annie
along with all my family and friends who contributed in many ways.

Elaine and Tom Bender, Bill Muzzillo, Jim Tamblyn

To Fran Breitner for all her help with research, preparation
and tasting all these recipes. She is a gem.

And to Gary Raschke,
whose expertise in art direction is absolutely amazing.
Just when I think we have done it all,
he goes and does something even more amazing.

To Rick Luettke, absolutely, the best photographer.

To Karen Barentzen, Beth Baroncini, Cathie Logan, Kelly Kelley,
Denise Grigg, Gina Bacardi, Tom Fratanuono, Serena Williams,
Roger Williams, Jeff Joyce, Brenda Bennett, Joe Mefferd
Greg Pax, Fran Brietner, Vicki Richardson, Amy Lewarchik,
Brooks Clayton, Sandy Shultz, Melissa Fleig and Emily West.

Finally to Libbey Glass, for giving me the opportunity to do what I enjoy doing.

Table of Contents

Introduction

Just Tasting Two is my second cookbook on mini appetizers, soups and salads that are perfect for tasting parties and any get together where you want to serve a variety of different foods in a small tasting fashion (very similar to Spanish Tapas). Little bits of this and that. Or as I stated in my first book, a trendy way to say you are invited over for a sampling of wonderful little appetizers, soups and salads that will be presented on little plates and in little bowls. I've adapted many new recipes that I have borrowed from friends and family that fit into these little containers. They make for a fabulous presentation, taste great and are easy as can be to prepare. All the ingredients can be found in any local grocery store or deli department.

Just Tasting Two is also about presentation. Each of these recipes can be made by itself, but a group of them together is what tasting is all about.

Today's consumers have fallen in love with the whole tasting party concept. Entertaining with small portions is fun and healthy.

Most of the following mini-tasting recipes are pretty quick and simple to make. Some do take a little longer, but none will take longer than 30 minutes to complete, which is important with today's lifestyles in home entertaining. So I've created another collection of recipes that will, hopefully, take the tasting party to new heights.

The glass and ceramic tasting party sets are available at most national retailers, especially at Bed, Bath & Beyond, Pier One Imports, JCPenneys, Home Outfitters, Meijers, Wegman's, Macy's and Krogers.

I hope you enjoy these wonderful little mini appetizers and soup recipes as much as I have enjoyed creating them. I have been using them for years.

Working in the tabletop industry has been very rewarding and it is where I have learned so much about entertaining. I love to entertain and I hope that Just Tasting Two with its mini appetizer and soup recipes will be a great way for you to turn your special occasion or cocktail party into something very special.

Enjoy !

Robert Zollweg

Containers, Preparation and Serving Suggestions

The following pages will show you a few easy steps in the preparation and serving of the mini tasting recipes, a few short cuts when time is so important and some tips on presentation to make this Tasting Party a fun and festive occasion for you and your guests.

My golden rule for entertaining is: "Always make your guests feel at home". Always have food and beverages that are common to your guests' tastes. Sometimes you can go just a little beyond to experiment, but not too far. They need to feel comfortable and you need to be relaxed and at ease for your enjoyment too. Parties should not be stressful, so keep it simple and casual. These recipes, along with your favorite mini-cocktails and desserts, will help guarantee a successful Tasting Party. Enjoy !

When it comes to containers in which to serve all these new appetizers, your choices are endless. Photographed below are some of the glass and ceramic containers I use to show-off these delicious tasting recipes in this cookbook. There are many wonderful containers in the marketplace that can be used to serve any of these tasting recipes. Tall shooter glasses make wonderful containers for cold soups and gelatin salads. Small ceramic ramekins and shot glasses work great for hot soups. Small mini bowls or plates are great for tasting appetizers. My only suggestion on serving containers is that they be small or mini. Tasting is about small bites of a variety of different appetizers, soups and salads, along with small portions of your favorite desserts and cocktails.

Containers

Preparation

Getting Ready

I usually do 3-4 different appetizers at one time. I get all the ingredients out on my kitchen counter, organize my table and have all small ingredients in small bowls or plastic storage bags. I cut up all the different ingredients if I can ahead of time. Just remember what ingredients go with what recipe. Get the easier recipes out of the way first, then tackle the more complicated ones. Better yet, have someone help you. It's more fun working together, anyways.

Serving Presentations

This elaborate tasting party is just what you need to show off your kitchen skills to your friends and family. Use a variety of mini appetizers on different platters and servers, add a few mini desserts and mini cocktails and you are ready to celebrate. You don't need this elaborate of a tasting party everytime you make a few tasting appetizers, but it is important to have a good variety or selection; otherwise it isn't a real tasting party.

Simple Appetizers

Greek Bruschetta

Bruschetta may sound Italian, but this one has a real Greek twist: delicious feta cheese and spices served on a crispy garlic toasted baguette. You will need a long narrow platter for a festive serving presentation. See photo at right.

1- 24" loaf of fresh, hard crusted french baguette, thinly sliced
1/2 stick of butter or margarine
some garlic salt
1 cup of crumbled feta cheese
1 Vidalia onion, finely chopped
1/4 cup finely chopped fresh cilantro or parsley
some sliced black olives
1 tbsp olive oil
1 tsp balsamic vinegar

Slice the French bread into 1/2" diagonal slices, on a severe angle, to expose more of the wonderful crust. Spread a little butter on each piece of bread. Sprinkle with a little garlic salt. Toast in broiler until golden brown. Remove from broiler and cool slightly.

In a mixing bowl, combine the crumbled feta cheese, chopped onion, cilantro and the sliced black olives. Toss with a little olive oil and balsamic vinegar. Place about a tablespoon of the feta cheese mixture on each piece of toast and spread around. Place on a really cool serving platter and Enjoy !

Ham & Asparagus Wraps

 These are not the traditional styled wraps, but more like roll-ups served in a little more unusual way. I like serving them in small juice like glasses for another unusual presentation.

You will need 5 or 6 of these tumblers. See photo at right.

12 fresh asparagus spears, trim off tough ends
1/4 cup salad dressing or mayonnaise
2 oz cream cheese, softened
1 tbsp spicy mustard
1 tsp chopped fresh thyme leaves
12 slices cooked deli ham, thinly sliced

In a microwaveable baking dish, cook the asparagus until crisp. Depending on your microwave, usually about 2 minutes. Do not overcook. Drain and let cool.

In a mixing bowl, mix together the mayonnaise, cream cheese, mustard and thyme. Spread about a teaspoon of this mixture over each slice of ham just to the edges. Roll the ham strip tightly around each piece of asparagus. Stack in an air tight container and refrigerate until chilled. Place 3-4 wraps in a small juice glass for an unusual presentation or place on a long rectangular platter. Serve and Enjoy !

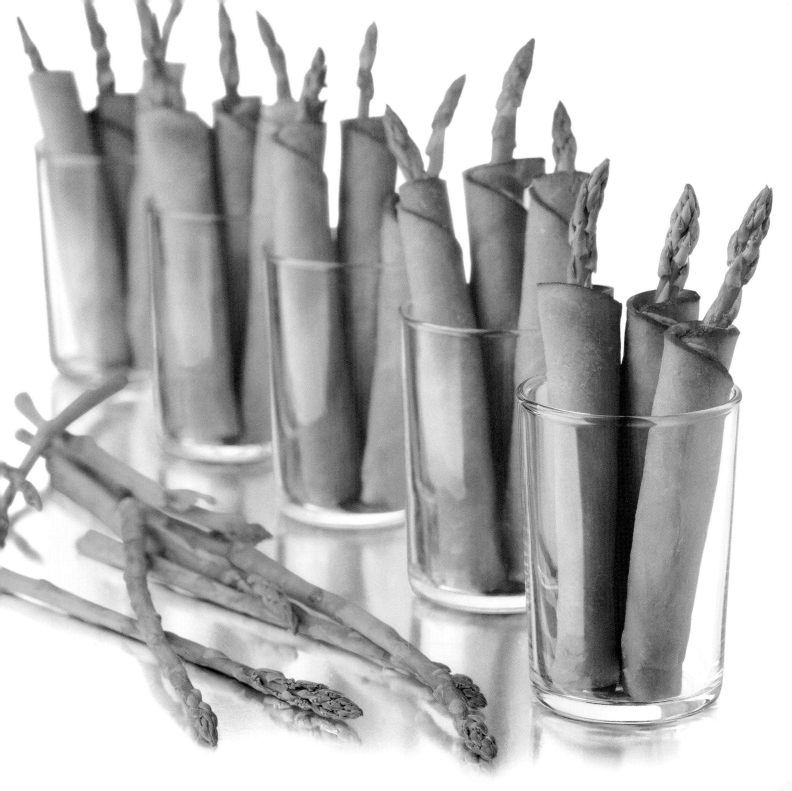

Tortellini Kabobs

These kabobs are different from what you may be used to, but you will find them very tasty, delicious and very vegetarian. This recipe is easy to expand by just increasing the quantity of ingredients.

You will need 12 mini appetizer plates for serving. See photo at right.

24 uncooked refrigerated or dried cheese filled spinach tortellini
1/2 cup Italian or balsamic salad dressing
12 small whole mushrooms, can use pieces of larger ones
12 small cherry tomatoes
12 black olives or green olives or both
12 bamboo skewers (6 inches long)

Cook and drain the tortellini as directed on the package. Cool about 15 minutes.

In mixing bowl, combine the Italian dressing, chilled tortellinis, mushrooms, black olives and cherry tomatoes. Let stand covered in the refrigerator for an hour or so, stirring occasionally.

Drain the mixture and save. On each skewer, place a tortellini, mushroom, tomato, black olive and another tortellini. Drizzle with the dressing and serve. Enjoy !

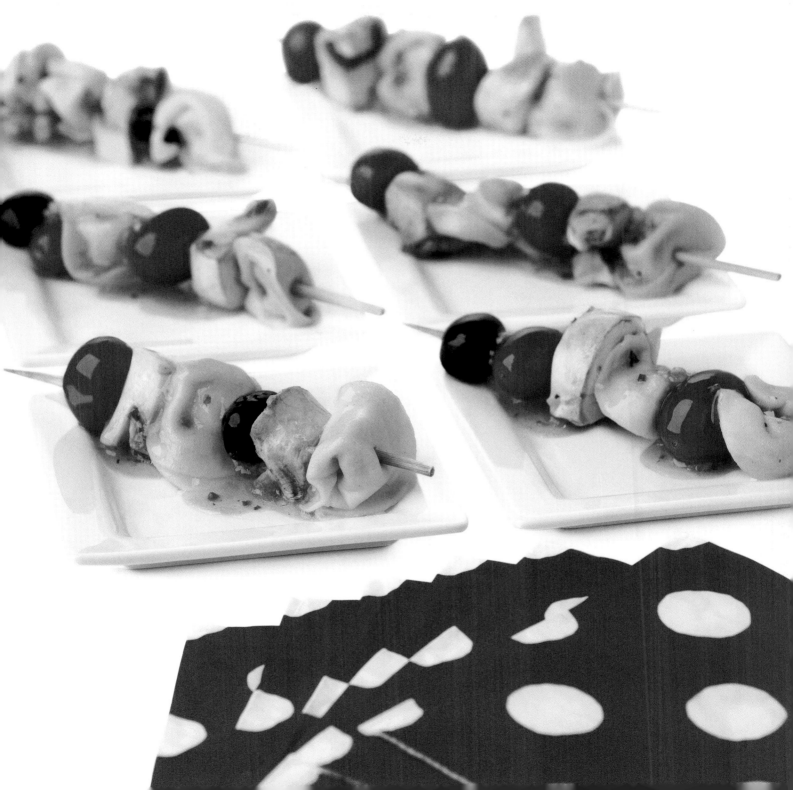

Cheesey Fruit Tasters

There are two different ways to prepare this recipe. They taste the same but are served differently (a wonderful combination of fresh fruit and cream cheese).

You will need 12 mini footed dessert dishes. See photo at right.

12 crackers (Ritz, Triscuit, Club, etc.)
1 - 8 oz package cream cheese, softened
1 cup sliced strawberries
1 cup sliced kiwi
1 cup pineapple chunks or small pieces
1 tbsp sugar
some pineapple juice

In a small mixing bowl combine the cream cheese, sugar and pineapple juice until smooth and creamy. In a zip lock bag, add the crackers and crush into small pieces. Cover the bottom of each dish with cracker pieces. Add a layer or large dollop of the cream mixture. Now add the fresh fruit on top of the cream cheese. It's that simple and that quick. Serve and Enjoy !

For a "pick up" appetizer, do not crush the crackers. Spread each whole cracker with a spoonful of cream cheese mixture from above. Add a piece of kiwi, strawberry and pineapple. Place on a beautiful serving tray and Enjoy !

Cucumber Feta Appetizer

Here's a treat that is light, refreshing and perfect for a warm summer day when you don't want to spend the whole day in the kitchen. Below are two different ways to prepare this recipe. Both use the same ingredients but one is a wrap and the other is a small salad that requires a cocktail fork.

You will need 12 small tasting dishes or a long cool platter. See photo at right.

3 cucumbers   8 oz crumbled feta cheese
4 tbsp plain yogurt   12 green olives, chopped
1 tbsp dried dill or oregano   black pepper to taste
1 tbsp lemon juice   several toothpicks
4 tbsp orange or red bell pepper or sun dried tomatoes, finely chopped

For the Cucumber Feta Wraps: Thinly slice the cucumbers the longway, about 1/8" thick. Lay strips on a piece of paper towel. In a mixing bowl, combine the yogurt and feta cheese and mash with a fork. Add the chopped peppers, olives, dill, lemon juice. Stir well. Place a tablespoon of the cheese mixture at the end of the cucumber strip and roll up. Secure with a toothpick. Repeat with remaining strips. Serve on a platter and Enjoy !

For the Cucumber Feta Salad: Chop the cucumbers into small bite size pieces. Add a spoonful of the cheese mixture from wrap recipe to the bottom of each small tasting dish. Add a layer of chopped cucumber on top. Garnish with some finely chopped red bell peppers or sun dried tomatoes. Serve and Enjoy !

Honey Cheddar Drizzle

The combination of honey, dates and cheese will be a wonderful sensation to your palette. I like to serve this in small tasting bowls as individual appetizers. It's a great presentation for a tasting buffet.

You will need 12 small tasting bowls for serving. See photo at right.

16 oz extra sharp cheddar cheese or aged swiss cheese
1/4 cup honey
1/2 cup pecans or walnuts, chopped
1/2 cup chopped dates
1 apple, sliced for garnish

This can be made with almost any good quality cheese. I prefer Swiss or Mozzarella cheese, but a lot of my friends like a sharper cheese. It is really up to your individual tastes.

Cut the cheese in 1/2" square pieces. Place several pieces in each small bowl. Sprinkle with the pecans and dates and drizzle with some honey. Garnish with an apple slice on the side. Serve and Enjoy !

Cucumber Bites

Here's a perfect appetizer when you are in a hurry and need something refreshing and quick. It's a rather healthy appetizer that is low in calories and carbs. I always have a plateful along with other appetizers at my tasting parties.

1 - 8 oz package cream cheese, softened
1 carrot, finely shredded
1 tbsp finely chopped onion
1 tbsp finely chopped chives
1 tsp dill weed
2 cucumbers (I prefer the English variety)
small jar of green olives, sliced, for garnish
some fresh ground black pepper

For something a little different, try adding chopped olives or dill pickles.

In a mixing bowl, combine the cream cheese, carrots, chives, dill weed and onions. Mix well and set aside.

Cut the cucumbers lengthwise. Remove the seeds. Fill each cucumber half with a few spoonfuls of cream cheese mixture and top with a few carrot pieces. Sprinkle with just a little black pepper. Then cut again in 1" length or chunks. Garnish each piece with a slice of green olive. Serve on a platter and you are ready to go. Enjoy !

Beefy Cheese Bites

Using beef makes this appetizer a little more hearty. It is an ideal appetizer when you need something a little more substantial. It can also be made with ham or deli turkey. I use cucumber in the center, but try avocado if you like.

You will need 12 small tasting dishes or a long platter. See photo at right.

12 slices of deli roast beef, medium thickness
1 package (8 oz) cream cheese, softened
1 tsp of garlic-herb spices
1/2 cup finely chopped red bell pepper
1/4 cup bacon bits or fresh crumbled bacon
1 cucumber
black pepper to taste

In a small mixing bowl, combine the cream cheese and spices. Cut the cucumber, the long way, in long thin strips. Take a slice of beef and lie it flat on a cutting board. Spread it with about a spoonful of cream cheese mixture. Add a strip of cucumber to fit the length of roast beef. Sprinkle with bell pepper, bacon bites and pepper to taste. Carefully roll up. Cut each roll into pieces, about 2-3 per roll up. Place 3-4 pieces in each tasting dish or all of them on a large serving platter. Serve and Enjoy !

Deviled Egg Parfait

This Deviled Egg Parfait is quite unique and different. My family has always loved deviled eggs, so I came up with something a little different than the traditional deviled egg that is cut in half, etc. This one is layered and served in a mini wine cordial or very small footed goblet.

You will need 12 mini wine glasses or cordials. See photo at right.

12 hard boiled eggs, peeled
1/4 cup sour cream
2 tbsp mayonnaise
2 tsp spicy mustard
1 tsp lemon juice
1/2 cup chopped tomatoes
1/2 cup of sliced green or black olives
1/4 cup cooked bacon, chopped
1/4 cup green onions, chopped
salt and coarse black pepper to taste
some chopped parsley or thyme for garnish

Cut each egg in half lengthwise. Drop half the egg into the cordial.

In a small mixing bowl, combine the sour cream, lemon juice, mayonnaise and spicy mustard. Blend well. Place a large spoonful of the cream mixture on top of the egg. Sprinkle with chopped bacon, green onions, tomatoes and olives (leaving enough sliced olives for garnish). Salt and pepper to taste.

Add the second half of the egg on top and then a small dollop of cream mixture and an olive slice for garnish. Sprinkle with parsley or thyme. Serve and Enjoy !

Figs & Honey Spread

This is another one of those wonderful creamy cheese appetizers that is perfect for a light snack while watching TV. It is also a perfect compliment to other delicious appetizers for a tasting party, especially when served with a glass of Chardonnay.

You will need 12 small mini tasting plates or dishes. See photo at right.

1 - 8 oz package cream cheese, softened
1/2 cup dried figs, finely chopped
1/4 cup basil, slice into strips
1/4 cup honey
1 tsp lemon juice or lemon zest
1 tsp sugar
black pepper
lots of small crackers (Triscuit, Club, Ritz, Wheat Thins, etc.)

In a mixing bowl combine cream cheese, 1/4 cup chopped figs, lemon juice, half the basil, the sugar and a dash of black pepper. Mix well.

Add a large spoonful of cream cheese mixture into each small square tasting dish. Add some dried figs and basil to each. Drizzle with honey and a dash of black pepper. Serve with several crackers on the side of each dish. Enjoy !

Mini Chicken Kabobs

This is another one of my favorites. I love the tangy sweet taste of the glaze along with the sweet pineapple. This is also very good cooked on the grill for a few minutes. Either way, they are delicious. You will need at least 24-36 cocktail toothpicks and a beautiful long serving tray or several tasting plates. See photo at right.

4 fresh chicken breasts, skinned, boned and cut into cubes
some olive or vegetable oil
1/2 cup dark brown sugar
1 tsp soy sauce
1 tbsp margarine or butter, melted
1 cup of pineapple chunks, fresh or canned (save the juice)
1 cup of fresh mango or cantaloupe, cubed
1 large green or red pepper, cut into large pieces
handful of toothpicks

In a mixing bowl, combine the dark brown sugar, soy sauce, butter and a little of the pineapple juice, mix well, set aside.

In a large skillet, with a little oil, cook the chicken pieces until done. They should have some nice brown color on the edges. Add some of the brown sugar glaze and toss until coated. Remove from pan. Set aside and let cool.

Taking a cocktail toothpick, start with a piece of pineapple, then the red or green pepper, a piece of chicken and end with pineapple, mango or green pepper or both, depending on the length of your cocktail pick. Layer the kabobs on a long serving platter and then drizzle with the remaining brown sugar glaze over all the kabobs. Serve and Enjoy !

Mexican Roll-Ups

This may not be the spiciest or most original Mexican appetizer around, but the unique combination of vegetables and spices has always made it a real crowd pleaser at my get togethers. Making it spicier is pretty simple; just add a little more spicy salsa or cayenne pepper. The different flavors or colors of tortillas also add a lot of pizzazz to the presentation.

You will need 12 small tasting plates or bowls for serving. See photo at right.

1 package cream cheese, 8 oz, softened
1/2 cup sour cream
2 tbsp taco seasoning mix
1/2 cup frozen corn, thawed
1/2 cup black beans, rinsed and drained
1/2 cup chopped tomatoes, seeded
1/4 cup chopped fresh cilantro
3 tbsp chunky salsa, mild, medium or hot
4 large plain flour tortillas, spinach, tomato or plain

1 cup of cooked, shredded chicken can be added as an option.

In a small mixing bowl, combine the cream cheese, sour cream and taco seasoning. Mix well. Stir in the corn, beans, cilantro, tomatoes and salsa. Blend well.

Spread a large heaping spoonful of the vegetable cream mixture over each tortilla to the edges. Add the shredded chicken if you choose. Roll up and wrap each one individually in plastic wrap and refrigerate for an hour or so. When ready to serve, cut with a sharp knife into 1" slices and place several on each tasting dish or several on a large platter. Serve and Enjoy !

Mini Caprese Cups

Here's a little taste of Italy with a different twist, but with lots of flavor. Nothing is more colorful on a tasting table than these Mini Caprese Cups. They are quick, easy and very delicious. Six simple ingredients will make a delicious appetizer that your guests will just love and compliment everything else on the tasting buffet.

You will need 12 small square tasting bowls. See photo at right.

36 large cherry tomatoes, cut in half
6 oz fresh mozzarella cheese, cut into small 1/2" cubes
1/2 cup black olives, sliced
1/2 cup Italian or Balsamic Vinaigrette Dressing
small bunch of basil leaves, chopped
some fresh ground coarse black pepper

In a mixing bowl, toss the cherry tomatoes, sliced black olives and cheese cubes with the salad dressing until well coated. Add the chopped basil and mix well. Drizzle a little more dressing over each tasting dish. Sprinkle with coarse black pepper. Place the small tasting bowls on a larger square platter. Serve and Enjoy !

Chicken with Mango Salsa

This is one of my favorite ways to serve grilled chicken for a tasting party. The mango salsa adds a kind of Brazilian flair to the chicken. I like to serve it on these wonderful tasting spoons, see photo at right. For another interesting presentation, serve this in small individual square dishes with some small cocktail forks. Either way, I think your guests will love them.

You will need 12 small tasting dishes or 12 ceramic spoons. See photo at right.

4 boneless chicken breasts, grilled and cooked thoroughly, cubed
1 mango, peeled and finely cubed
12 oz fresh pineapple, diced or canned pineapple tidbits
1/2 cup red pepper, finely chopped
1/2 cup green pepper, finely chopped
1/2 cup honey, divided in half
4-5 fresh basil leaves, chopped
2 tsp red pepper flakes

In a larger mixing bowl, combine the mango, pineapple, chopped basil and red and green peppers, 1 tsp red pepper flakes and 1/4 cup of the honey, mix well. Place a heaping spoonful of the mango salsa in the bottom of each mini spoon.

In a small mixing bowl, place the other half of the honey and 1 tsp. red pepper flakes. Dip the grilled chicken cubes into the honey. Place 1-2 chicken cubes in each individual serving spoon on top of the mango salsa, drizzle with any left over honey-pepper sauce.

Refrigerate until ready to serve. Enjoy !

Mango Ham Salsa

This is a very interesting appetizer that comes out quite delicious and different. It's not really a salsa but more like a mini salad. I've used it on top of grilled chicken and it's delicious. Just serve it by itself on these wonderful tasting spoons.

You will need 12 mini tasting bowls or ceramic spoons for serving. See photo at right.

2 ripe mangos, peeled and cubed
2 cups chopped ham
1 cup cantaloupe, chopped
1/4 cup honey
1 tbsp brown sugar
splash of balsamic vinegar

In a large mixing bowl, combine the honey, brown sugar and balsamic vinegar. Mix well. Add the chopped mangos, ham and cantaloupe and mix until well coated. Place a heaping spoonful in each tasting dish. Serve and Enjoy !

Spicy Asian Avocado Shrimp

This is a kind of salad appetizer but could also be used for a light entree for brunch. It does not need to be real spicy, but will depend on your tastes and how much hot sauce you use. I love it for a get together along with some chicken kabobs and a light dessert.

You will need 12 mini tasting dishes. See photo at right.

36 small shrimp, tails removed
1 tbsp lime zest
2 springs of fresh mint, chopped
1/4 cup shredded carrots
3 oz (1/3 cup) bean sprouts, chopped
3 oz (1/3 cup) glass noodles, cooked and rinsed with cold water, then chopped
6 Bibb lettuce leaves, shredded
3 oz sesame vinaigrette

2 tbsp lime juice
1 tbsp hot sauce
4 avocados, chopped
2 tbsp fresh basil, chopped

pinch of salt

Preheat oven to 325 degrees. In a rectangular baking dish, combine shrimp, lime juice and lime zest, hot sauce, mint and a pinch of salt. Toss together. Bake for 7-8 minutes. Let cool and refrigerate.

In the bottom of each tasting bowl, place a layer of shredded Bibb lettuce, about a heaping tablespoon full.

In a mixing bowl, gently toss together the noodles, sprouts, avocado, carrots with the sesame vinaigrette. Mix in the shrimp or just place several shrimp on each dish. Fill each dish until full. Sprinkle with chopped basil. Serve and Enjoy !

Veggie Sushi

Sushi is all about the rice and the ingredients that goes with it. This is a simple vegetable sushi. These mini Sushi dishes are perfect for something a little different to add to your tasting party assortment.

You will need 12 small glass dipping bowls. See photo at right.

2 cups sushi rice (not long grain or instant)
2 cups water   2 tbsp sushi or rice vinegar
2 tsp sugar   1 tsp salt

1 bunch of asparagus, sliced and chopped
2-3 scallions or green onions   1 yellow bell pepper, thinly sliced
1 ripe avocado, peeled and pitted   3-4 whole carrots, sliced and chopped
4-5 radishes, chopped   black sesame seeds for garnish, optional
some soy sauce   some wasabi paste

Rinse the sushi rice several times. Put the rice in a saucepan with 2 cups water. Cover tightly and bring to boil, reduce heat and simmer until all water is absorbed, about 15 minutes. Leave covered and set aside, let cool. Fluff with a fork. Mix together the vinegar, sugar and salt. Sprinkle over the rice. Cover rice until ready to use.

Microwave the asparagus, radishes and carrots until slightly tender.

Fill your small bowls with a 1/4" layer of rice. Flatten (a little water on the tip of your finger works well). Add a layer of finely chopped vegetables of your choice from above. Sprinkle with soy sauce. Add another layer of rice and flatten down a little. Garnish the top with carrots, bell pepper and sprinkle with sesame seeds. Serve with a side dipping bowl of wasabi paste and soy sauce. Enjoy !

Hot Appetizers

Spinach Artichoke Pizzas

This recipe will make about 20 wonderful little Sicilian style pizzas. These are really delicious little tarts that are good hot or cold. You will need a couple of cup cake or muffin tins to bake them in and several mini tasting plates or a large flat serving platter. See photo at right.

Preheat oven to 425 degrees

1 pkg. refrigerator rolls or biscuits
1 (10 oz) box of frozen chopped spinach, thawed
1 (14 oz) can or jar artichoke hearts, drained and chopped
1 cup red and yellow bell peppers, finely chopped
2 cups parmesan cheese
1 cup sour cream
1 (8 oz) package cream cheese, softened
1/3 cup mayonnaise
1 tsp minced garlic

Spray each of the muffin pans with nonstick cooking spray. Unroll the refrigerator rolls and separate. Cut each roll in half and flatten in the bottom of the muffin pan. Press down. Set aside.

In a large mixing bowl, combine the parmesan cheese, bell peppers, spinach and artichoke hearts. Set aside.

In another larger mixing bowl, combine the sour cream, mayonnaise and cream cheese and garlic, mix well. Add the spinach-artichoke mixture and mix well. Place a heaping spoonful on top of each biscuit. Spread it around. Bake in the oven at 425 degrees for 12-15 minutes or until golden brown. Cool slightly and remove from pan. Can be served hot or at room temperature. Arrange on a beautiful oval platter or on individual tasting plates. Serve and Enjoy !

Pizza Mediterranean

This pizza recipe is a little more like the old world pizzas from Italy. It's not your typical pizza from the United States because youl don't use tomato sauce. It's just a wonderful combination of cheeses, spices and flavors, and wonderful in the summer with a glass of Pinot Grigio or a nice Chianti.

This will make about 20 small 3" individual pizzas. See photo at right.

Preheat oven to 425 degrees

4-5 large ripe tomatoes   1 cup fresh mozzarella cheese
1/2 cup parmesan cheese   some olive oil
1 pkg refrigerator biscuits   some oregano or Italian seasoning
one yellow or red bell pepper, chopped

If you like garlic flavor, add a little garlic salt to the olive oil and oregano

Remove biscuits from the tube, separate and cut in half. Roll in a ball and then flatten on a cookie sheet. This should make about twenty mini pizzas. Brush the crusts with a little olive oil and sprinkle with oregano or Italian seasoning and parmesan cheese.

Cut the tomatoes into very thin slices. Place a slice of tomato on each individual crust. Sprinkle with mozzarella cheese and some chopped bell peppers.

Bake for about 12-15 minutes until crispy brown. Arrange on a platter and serve. Enjoy !

Spicy Meatballs

Meatballs are one of those versatile appetizers that can be served warm or at room temperature. They're perfect for a tasting party. For a fabulous presentation, you will need 12 small appetizer plates. Add a small shot glass full of toothpicks for your guests to spear the meatballs or use some small cocktail forks. See photo at right.

2 lbs fresh ground pork or beef, or a combination of both
1 cup bread crumbs, from crusty bread
1 large onion, finely chopped
1 garlic glove, crushed
2 tbsp fresh parsley, finely chopped
1 egg, beaten
pinch of nutmeg, salt and pepper
some flour for coating meatballs
1 tbsp Italian spices
2 tbsp olive oil

Sauce
2 tbsp olive oil
1/2 cup chopped almonds
1 tsp red pepper flakes
1 garlic clove, crushed
2/3 cup white wine
1 cup beef or vegetable broth
1/4 cup green onions, chopped

In a large mixing bowl, add ground pork or beef, chopped onion, garlic, parsley. Mix thoroughly. Add beaten egg, nutmeg, salt and pepper. Mix well. Form mixture into small balls. Roll each of them in a little flour. In a large skillet, add a little oil and cook several meatballs at a time for 4-5 minutes or so until brown. Work in batches.

To make the spicy sauce, heat 2 tbsp olive oil (if needed) in the same skillet in which the meatballs were cooked, removing any extra grease. Add almonds and saute a few minutes. Add garlic, pepper flakes and green onions, cook a few more minutes. Add white wine, beef broth and the spices. Simmer at least 10-15 minutes.

Return the meatballs to the sauce in the skillet and cook on low heat for 30 minutes or so. Season with salt and pepper. Place 2-3 meatballs on each small plate and add a teaspoon of sauce over the meatballs. Serve and Enjoy !

Mini Party Quiches

These are great little quiches for a brunch or morning breakfast and can be made with almost any added ingredient (mushrooms, green pepper, tomatoes, etc.).

You will need 20 small, 3 oz ramekins, suitable for baking. See photo at right.

Preheat oven to 350 degrees

5 eggs, beaten	1 cup cottage cheese
1/4 cup flour	1/2 tsp baking powder
1/4 cup butter or margarine, melted	4 tbsp finely chopped green onions
2 cups grated Monterey Jack cheese	1 pkg refrigerator biscuits
1/4 cup cheddar cheese, shredded	one jar of salsa for topping, optional

You can add almost anything to this recipe, bacon, mushrooms, green pepper, etc.

Separate the biscuits and cut in half. Roll in little balls. Place a pastry ball in each ramekin, press down. Bake for 10 minutes at 350 degrees, until just brown and slightly puffy. Press these down once cooled a little.

You can make this quiche without the pastry crust or use a layer of toasted bread cubes as a bottom crust.

In a large bowl, combine beaten eggs and cottage cheese. Beat in flour, baking powder and melted butter. Stir in Monterey Jack cheese and green onions. Mix well. Pour mixture equally into the ramekins. Sprinkle a few pieces of cheddar cheese on top, optional. Bake at 350 degrees for 20 minutes or until done. Serve warm, plain or with salsa on the side in a small bowl. Enjoy !

Cheese Dip Singles

This is a wonderful cheesy chicken recipe that works as a dip with chips or as an entree all by itself. It can be made with a little more zing just by adding some hot sauce. This makes a great cheese dip with no worrying about double dipping.

You will need 12 small ramekins or mini tasting dishes that are suitable for baking. See photo at right.

Preheat oven to 350 degrees

8 oz cream cheese, softened
1 cup shredded cooked chicken
1/2 cup ranch salad dressing
1/2 cup salsa or enchilada sauce
1/2 cup shredded mozzarella cheese

In a large mixing bowl, combine the cream cheese and ranch dressing. Add the salsa, shredded mozzarella cheese and shredded chicken. Mix well. Fill each of the small baking dishes and place on a cookie sheet. Bake at 350 degrees for 15-20 minutes or until heated through. Serve immediately. Served with some toasted chips, crackers or by itself.

You can also add a dollop of salsa on top right before serving, optional.

Serve and Enjoy !

Barbecue Sausage Kabobs

This is the perfect tasting party food that will appeal to both guys and gals. The zingy and spicy taste of barbecue together with spicy sausages, is dee-licious !

You will need 12 small tasting plates for individual servings or a long platter for stacking them high. See photo at right.

Preheat oven to 325 degrees

1-1/2 cups barbecue sauce	1/2 cup orange marmalade
1/2 cup dark brown sugar	1 tsp mustard
1/8 tsp allspice	24-30 cocktail toothpicks (4 inch)
1 lb cooked bratwursts	1 lb cooked kielbasa
1 lb cooked sausage links	1 can of pineapple chunks or fresh pineapple

In a mixing bowl, combine the barbecue sauce, marmalade, brown sugar, mustard and allspice. Mix well. Cut all the sausage links in 1/2" slices or chunks.

Take a long toothpick and place a piece of each of the different types of sausage along with a pineapple chunk in the middle. Dip the kabobs into the barbecue sauce and lay on a cookie sheet (I cover the cookie sheet with foil for easier cleanup). Bake in the oven for 15-20 minutes, or until they brown a little. These are also great cooked on an outdoor grill. Place 2-3 kabobs on each tasting plate or on a large serving platter and drizzle with remaining barbecue sauce. Serve and Enjoy !

Ratatouille el Mediterranean

Here's another perfect side dish to serve along with all the other tasting appetizers. It could almost be a meal in itself, because it is so hearty. It's a great vegetarian dish and delicious served hot or cold.

You will need 12 small tasting bowls, suitable for baking. See photo at right.

Preheat oven to 350 degrees (this can also be microwaved)

1/2 cup finely chopped onions
1 tbsp olive oil
1/2 cup green pepper, chopped

1 tsp minced garlic
1 large potato, cubed
salt and pepper

2 cups eggplant, peeled and cubed
1 zucchini, cut in pieces
1 cup whole tomatoes, cut up or stewed tomatoes
2 tbsp white wine or water
1 tsp dried basil or 1 tbsp fresh basil, chopped
1/2 cup swiss cheese, shredded

In a large microwaveable bowl, combine the onions, garlic, olive oil, green peppers and potatoe cubes. Microwave for about 5 minutes until everything is a little tender. In the same bowl, add the remaining ingredients except the Swiss cheese. Toss until well coated and mixed well. Fill each of the small baking bowls with the ratatouille.

Bake in the oven for 25 minutes or until vegetables are tender. Or cook in the microwave for about 10-12 minutes. Then sprinkle with Swiss cheese and bake another 5 minutes or microwave for 1-2 minutes until cheese starts to melt. Serve and Enjoy !

Baked Mushrooms

A delicious dish of baked mushrooms is all you need to put together a wonderful start to a tasting party. The combination of mushrooms, feta cheese and pine nuts will put you r party over the top. It's a wonderful compliment to any meat course.

You will need 12 small baking dishes. See photo at right.

Preheat oven to 400 degrees

1 lb small white or Portobello mushrooms
4 oz (3/4 cup) feta or goat cheese, crumbled and divided
1/2 cup pine nuts, toasted
1/3 cup chopped onion
2 tbsp olive oil
2 tsp minced garlic
1/2 tsp oregano
1/8 tsp black pepper

Wipe the mushrooms with a damp cloth to clean and cut into bite size pieces.

In a large mixing bowl, combine the onions, garlic and olive oil. Stir in the pine nuts, oregano and black pepper. Mix until well blended. Add the mushroom pieces, feta cheese and mix well. Spoon mushroom mixture into each small baking dish. Sprinkle with some extra feta cheese. Bake in oven for 20-25 minutes or until heated through. Serve and Enjoy !

Sausage Cheese Pie

This is a whole meal in itself and will make a great compliment to some of the other side dish recipes for any tasting party.

You will need 12 small baking dishes, see photo at right.

Preheat oven to 400 degrees

1 lb bulk Italian sausage	1 onion, chopped, about a 1/2 cup
1 red or green bell pepper, chopped	1 tsp minced garlic
1 can (15 oz) tomato sauce	1 package (10 oz) frozen corn, thawed
1/2 cup chopped mushrooms	1/2 cup shredded cheddar cheese

One package corn bread mix.

Cook sausage, onion, bell pepper and garlic in a skillet over medium heat until it is no longer pink, drain. Stir in tomato sauce, corn and mushrooms. Cook for about 10 minutes or heated through. Remove from heat.

Fill each of the small baking dishes about 3/4 full. Add a spoonful of cheese on top.

Prepare the corn bread as directed. Spoon a large, heaping spoonful of corn bread mixture on top of the sausage mixture to cover the top. Bake for about 20-25 minutes or until golden brown. Serve and Enjoy !

Baked Taco Pie

What could have more of a Mexican flare than Taco Pie? It's a really great appetizer when served with other complimenting foods, like Mexican Roll-Ups or Mango Gazpacho Soup. Make a pitcher of margaritas and you are ready to sit back and enjoy some good times with friends and family.

You will need 12 small baking dishes, see photo at right.

Preheat oven to 400 degrees

1 lb lean ground beef
1 package of taco seasoning mix
1-1/2 cups milk
1 cup cheddar cheese, shredded
1 tomato, thinly sliced for garnish

1 medium onion, chopped
1 cup Bisquick Original baking mix
3 eggs
3 tomatoes, finely chopped, divided
1/4 cup of sliced black olives

In a large skillet, cook the ground beef and onions until brown, drain. Stir in the taco seasoning mix. Add half the chopped tomatoes. Fill each of the small baking dishes with this mixture about 3/4 full, leaving room at the top for the Bisquick mix.

In a mixing bowl, combine the baking mix, milk and eggs. Whisk for a minute or two. Pour a heaping spoonful of mixture over the ground beef to cover the top.

Bake for 25 minutes or so until knife inserted comes out clean. Remove from oven and immediately sprinkle with the shredded cheese. Return to oven for a minute or so until cheese melts a little. Cool a few minutes. Garnish with tomato slice and black olives. Serve and Enjoy !

Party Soups

City Bean Soup

Bean soup is bean soup, but if you live in the city, you look for short cuts to make a great hearty soup fast. It's great for parties or get togethers. The trick here is to make it the night before. This will make more than enough to fill 12 small tasting bowls. You will need 12 mini-soup dishes or bowls 3-4 oz each. See photo at right.

a large ham bone or several slices or chunks of ham
bay leaf
several stalks of celery, cut up
a couple of carrots, sliced
one small onion, cut up
8 cups of water

2 large ham slices, cubed
1 can stewed or diced tomatoes
one large jar of Randell's multi-beans
one large jar of Randell's navy beans
1/2 cup instant mashed potatoes
some salt and pepper

Place the ham bone, bay leaf, celery, carrots and onion with the water in the stock pot and simmer for about 4-6 hours. Sometimes I do this the day before and let it sit overnight.

Remove bone and any fat. Add the cubed ham, tomatoes and juice, salt and pepper and all the beans and simmer for another hour or so. Add the instant mashed potatoes and stir thoroughly. This is really good when made the day before and reheated. Serve in little mini soup bowls for a cocktail party or wide rimmed soup bowls for dinner. Served with toasted french bread. Enjoy !

Fresh Asparagus Soup

There are asparagus lovers and non asparagus lovers; for the lovers of the world, this cream soup is for you. I love to serve it in mini bowls or these mini glass mugs as pictured when I'm doing a buffet. The small mini bowls or mugs give you just enough to compliment the other appetizers on your tasting table. You will need 12 mini soup bowls or mugs. See photo at right.

1 lb fresh asparagus, chopped
one small onion, chopped
3 cups chicken broth
2 stalks of celery, diced
pinch of salt and pepper
1 tsp lemon juice

4 tbsp of butter or margarine
3 tbsp flour
one sprig of fresh basil
pinch of cayenne pepper
1 cup half and half or heavy cream

In a heavy saucepan, place the chopped asparagus, celery, basil, onion and half chicken broth. Bring to boil. Reduce heat and simmer until vegetables are tender. Let cool. Place in a blender and puree until smooth. Set aside.

Melt butter in the same saucepan. Add flour, salt and pepper, cayenne pepper to make a roux, whisk in the remaining chicken broth. Simmer about 30 minutes. Add the pureed vegetable mixture, lemon juice and the half and half. Mix well and simmer another 15 minutes. Ladle into small tasting bowls or mugs and serve hot. See page 84.

Serve and Enjoy !

Apple Pumpkin Soup

Apple Pumpkin soup is one of my favorite soups to make in the fall. It's great served right before a hearty meal or in little mini bowls at a fall harvest buffet on a cool brisk night. This recipe makes more than enough for 12 servings in small deep glass or ceramic bowls, with plenty for later or the next day. To keep it hot, place the filled bowls on a cookie sheet and place in the oven at 200 degrees until ready to serve.

Serve in mini tasting bowls, about 4 oz.each, see photo at right.

1 can (15 oz) solid-pack pumpkin
4 cups of chicken broth
1/2 cup chopped onion
2 cups finely chopped peeled apples
2 cups whole milk
1 cup sour cream
2 tbsp butter or margarine
1/2 cup dark brown sugar
1/2 tsp each of cinnamon, nutmeg, ginger and gloves
salt and black pepper

In a large saucepan, saute the apples, onion and butter about 5 minutes or until tender. Mash with a potato masher or wooden spoon. Stir in flour until blended. Whisk in chicken broth until smooth. Stir in pumpkin, sour cream, milk, brown sugar and spices. Bring almost to a boil and then reduce heat and simmer for 20 minutes or so. Season with salt and pepper. Serve warm or hot in small bowls. Enjoy !

Cauliflower Cream Soup

Originally I got interested in cauliflower because it was low in carbohydrates. But I have acquired a taste for it and now think it is really quite unique and delicious. This is a wonderful cream soup that will compliment almost any buffet or tasting dinner party.

You will need 12 little individual ceramic ramekins or small bowls, see photo at right.

1 large head of cauliflower, leaves removed
1 carrot, peeled and chopped
2 stalks of celery, chopped
1 small onion, chopped
salt and black pepper

1 cup heavy cream or half and half
2 tbsp butter or margarine
3 cups chicken broth
1/4 cup white wine
pinch of nutmeg

(I've used whole milk instead of heavy cream or half and half, not quite as rich and creamy but probably a little more healthy.)

In a large pot over medium heat, cook the butter, carrot, onion and celery, stirring every so often, about 5 minutes or so. Add chicken broth. Bring to boil. Add the cauliflower pieces, cover and simmer until vegetables are tender, 10-20 minutes or so. You can also do all of these steps in a microwaveable bowl.

Puree the cooled vegetables in a food processor or blender. If you want your soup chunkier, do not process as long. Return to pot, add heavy cream, salt, pepper, nutmeg and white wine. Simmer over medium heat until hot. Serve in some wonderful little ceramic or glass bowls or ramekins. Garnish with some croutons, dollop of sour cream or fresh parsley. Serve and Enjoy !

Tomato Basil Soup

There is nothing like fresh homemade tomato soup. Adding some fresh basil just gives it that extra flavor or zing. Sometimes I serve grilled cheese sandwiches cut into small triangles for a side. Crouton sticks are also a great compliment and perfect for dipping. See recipe below. You will have plenty of the tomato soup left over for lunch or dinner the next day.

You will need 12 small soup crocks. See photo at right.

1 large can (28 oz) of tomatoes	1 cup chicken broth
1/4 cup fresh basil, chopped	1 small onion, sliced
1 bay leaf	1 tsp sugar
1 tsp salt	1/4 tsp pepper
1 cup heavy cream	
1/4 cup sour cream or some croutons sticks on the side, optional	

In a food processor or blender, puree the tomatoes, basil and onion. Place mixture in a large saucepan. Add the chicken broth, sugar, salt and pepper. Simmer for 10 minutes. Stir in the heavy cream and simmer another 10 -15 minutes until hot, but do not boil. Serve in little tasting bowls. Drizzle a little sour cream or chopped basil on top and serve with crouton sticks. Enjoy !

Crouton Sticks

Take any left over thick bread and cut it into long 3" strips. Coat each side with butter or margarine and sprinkle lightly with Italian seasoning. Place on cookie sheet and broil for a few minutes on each side until golden brown. Let cool and serve.

Peach Mint Chilled Soup

Nothing is more refreshing than a chilled soup. This is another one of my favorites. It is a little on the sweet side, but with the combination of flavors, it is smooth as silk and equally as delicious. I love to serve it in little mini bowls because it is just the right amount to go along with a variety of other tasting appetizers.

You will need 12 mini dishes, about 4 oz each. See photo at right.

4 cups sliced peaches, drained and chopped
1/2 cup dark brown sugar
1/2 cup coconut milk
several sprigs of fresh mint for garnish

1 tbsp vegetable oil
2 cups vegetable broth
1/2 cups peach yogurt
4 tbsp chopped mint

In a large saucepan, heat the oil. Add the peaches and cook until peaches are softened, about 5 minutes. Stir in the brown sugar and vegetable broth and cook until sugar is dissolved, about 10 minutes. Let cool.

When cool, stir in coconut milk and 4 tbsp chopped mint.

Pour soup into a blender, cover and puree until smooth. Pour the pureed mixture into a large bowl and add the peach yogurt. Sometimes I will add the yogurt right in the blender. Mix well. Refrigerate until completely chilled. When ready to serve, ladle into small tasting bowls and garnish with a mint leaf. Serve and Enjoy !

Summer Mango Gazpacho Soup

This is a great soup for a summer get together, light, refreshing and very healthy. I love to serve it in these mini glass tumblers or mini bowls. It doesn't get any cooler than that. This recipe also makes quite a bit of soup, which is great, because it is even better the next day.

You will need 12-15 of these mini glass dishes. See photo at right.

2 cups diced fresh mango
2 cups orange juice
1 tbsp olive oil
1 cucumber, seeded and diced
1 small red bell pepper, diced
1 small onion, chopped

2 small garlic cloves, minced
3 tbsp lime juice
2 tbsp fresh parsley, chopped
2 tbsp fresh basil, chopped
salt and black pepper

For smooth soup: Use a food processor or a blender. Process the mango, orange juice and oil until pureed. Add the remaining ingredients and puree. Season with salt and pepper. Refrigerate until chilled. Serve in mini parfait shooters or mini bowls. Enjoy !

For chunky soup, use a large mixing bowl, add the pureed mango mixture to all the remaining finely chopped ingredients. Mix well. Season with salt and pepper. Refrigerate until chilled. Serve in mini parfait shooters or mini bowls. Enjoy !

Strawberry Chilled Soup

This is a wonderful soup that I serve when strawberries are at the height of their growing season and they are ripe and juicy. It is so light and refreshing. Perfect when served with a fresh garden salad and a glass of Pinot Grigio, and ideal for a summer brunch.

You will need 12 mini tasting bowls or any unusual small stem, like the photo at right.

2 pints fresh strawberries
2 cups vanilla yogurt
1/2 cup red wine
1/2 cup orange juice
1/2 cup white sugar

In a blender, combine the strawberries, yogurt, red wine, orange juice and sugar. Puree until smooth and creamy. Pour into a container and refrigerate until well chilled. When ready to serve, pour into any sleek mini cocktail glass or bowl and serve. Enjoy !

Tropical Chilled Soup

Follow the recipe from above but substitute fresh pineapple, peaches, mango, kiwi or papaya for the strawberries. Use white wine instead of red. Puree the orange juice, sugar and your fresh tropical fruit the same and refrigerate until well chilled. Serve in a really cool mini cocktail glass.

Also try just pineapple orange or pineapple mango or peach mango for a more distinctive taste. Serve and Enjoy !

Mini Salads

Festive Beet Salad

This salad will go with almost any meat entree, pork, turkey or chicken. Beets can sometimes seem heavy, but this recipe is very light and refreshing. It is a little tangy, not real sweet, and ideal for a vegetable compliment to your tasting buffet.

You will need 12 small glass dishes or bowls, about 3 oz each. See photo at right.

1 can (16 oz) beets, diced or julienne
2 packages lemon gelatin, 3 oz each
1-1/2 cups cold water
2 tbsp finely chopped onion
1/2 tsp horseradish
3 tsp white vinegar
1/4 tsp salt
1-1/2 cups celery, finely chopped
1/4 cup olives, sliced or chopped
some sour cream or yogurt for garnish, optional

Drain beets but reserve juice. Add water to juice to make 2 cups liquid, set beets aside. Place the 2 cups beet juice in a saucepan, bring to boil. Remove from heat and add the gelatin. Stir until completely dissolved. Add the 1 cup cold water, onion, horseradish, vinegar and salt. Refrigerate until jelled or partially set. Do not let completely set.

Stir in the celery, olives and chopped beets. Pour into the individual mini bowls. Chill until set, about 3 hours. Add a dollop of sour cream or yogurt for garnish. Serve and Enjoy !

Garden Stacker

This is a cute little salad that is perfect for a tasting party or outdoor picnic when you want something to look a little extra special for someone. You can use almost any combination of salad ingredients, whatever you like.

You will need 12 small tasting plates, square or round, see photo at right.

4 large ripe tomatoes, thinly sliced
12 oz Mozzarella or Swiss Cheese, thinly sliced
1/2 cup Italian or Balsamic salad dressing
2 large red onions, thinly sliced
1 large cucumber, thinly sliced
a bunch of fresh basil
fresh ground black pepper
4-5 black olives, sliced

For something a little more special, take the star or scalloped round cookie cutter and cut out the shape in the piece of cheese.

Place all your tasting plates on your counter. Place a tomato slice on each plate, followed by a slice of cheese, slice of onion, tomato, cheese and cucumber. I drizzle a little salad dressing after a layer or two and especially over the top. Sprinkle with fresh ground black pepper and garnish with some chopped basil and a slice or two of black olives.

Serve and Enjoy !

Apricot Orange Gelatin Salad

This is a great salad for a family get together. It is colorful and serving it in little mini dishes just adds to its uniqueness. This will make more than enough to fill 12 mini bowls, so have some extra or another large bowl for what is left.

You will need 12 small glass dishes, about 4 oz each. See photo at right.

32 oz canned apricot halves
6 oz package orange gelatin
1 can (6 oz) frozen orange juice concentrate, thawed
1/2 cup finely chopped celery
1/2 cup yellow bell pepper, finely chopped
1 tbsp lemon juice
dash of salt
1 cup lemon-lime soda

Drain apricots and set aside. Save the apricot juice. In a small saucepan, bring apricot juice (1-1/2 cups) and salt to boil. Remove from heat and add the orange gelatin, stirring until completely dissolved.

In a blender, combine the orange juice concentrate, lemon juice and apricot halves. Process until chunky.

In a large mixing bowl or pourable batter bowl, combine the gelatin mixture, lemon-lime soda, celery, bell peppers and the orange juice mixture. Mix well. Pour into the mini glass dishes and refrigerate until set, about 2-3 hours. Serve and Enjoy !

Papaya Mango Kiwi Fruit Salad

If the title of this recipe isn't a mouthful, wait until you taste this salad. It is completely the opposite, very light and refreshing and rather healthy.

You will need 12 mini tasting dishes, about 3 oz each. See photo at right.

2 papayas, peeled, seeded and sliced
2 mangos, peeled and sliced
2 kiwi fruits, peeled and sliced
1 orange
1 lime
3/4 cup sour cream
4 tbsp honey

You can cube the fresh fruit or cut it into julienne strips. Sometimes I add a small can of mandarin oranges for something different.

Grate the orange and lime to make about 2 tbsp of zest. Squeeze the juice from both the orange and lime into a large mixing bowl. Add the honey and mix well. Stir in the sour cream. Add the fresh fruit to the sour cream mixture and toss carefully. Divide the fruit mixture equally between the 12 dishes. Sprinkle with a little lime and orange zest. Serve and Enjoy !

Pineapple Gelatin Salad

This is a wonderful summer salad and has been in my family for years. My mother made it all the time when I was a kid for all of our special family get togethers. It is very light and refreshing and pretty simple to make. I like serving it in mini glass bowls because of the wonderful creamy green color.

You will need 12 or so small glass dishes. See photo at right.

1 box (6 oz) of lime gelatin
2 cups boiling water
1 cup cold water
1 container (8 oz) cottage cheese
1 can crushed pineapple, well drained

For something different, try lemon or orange gelatin instead of the lime.

In a microwavable bowl, add 2 cups water and microwave to a boil. Add lime gelatin and stir until dissolved, about 2 minutes. Add the 1 cup cold water. Stir well. Chill for about 30 minutes until it starts to jell, do not let set.

Stir in the cottage cheese and crushed pineapple, mix well. Fill each of the mini dishes with the gelatin mixture and refrigerate until set, about 1-2 hours. Serve and Enjoy !

Festive Olive Salad

This one is so simple and easy, and your guests will love it. Great for a cocktail party served with lots of mini martinis. You can use any assortment of olives. I've used green olives with pimentos and black olives. Today, there are many varieties of delicious and unusual olives that are available at your local supermarket.

You will need about 12 small appetizer bowls and a serving tray. See photo at right.

a jar of pimento stuffed green olives
a can of large pitted black olives
a chunk of mozzarella cheese
a chunk of Swiss cheese
one small sweet onion, chopped
balsamic vinegar
olive oil
salt and pepper
some Italian seasoning

Drain the olives and place in a mixing bowl. Take any kind of cheese you like and cut it into small cubes, about the size of the olives. Add the cheese cubes and chopped onion to the olives. Toss with some balsamic vinegar, olive oil, salt and pepper and some Italian seasoning.

Sometimes I add some small cherry tomatoes, cut in half. Serve in individual mini bowls with small cocktail forks.

Serve and Enjoy !

Watermelon Salad

This refreshing summer salad is perfect for those special holiday potlucks when everything is available fresh and right from the garden. Sometimes I even prepare it as a salsa dip. All I do is chopped everything a little finer. Either way, its delicious.

You will need 12 or so small glass bowls. See photo at right.

3 cups watermelon, cubed and seeds removed
1 cup coarsely chopped cucumber, cubed
1/2 cup chopped red onion
1/2 cup chopped red bell pepper
1/4 cup cilantro, chopped
2 tbsp basil, chopped
1 tbsp chopped green chilies
4 tbsp honey
1 tbsp lime juice

In a large mixing bowl, combine the watermelon cubes, cucumber, peppers, onions, cilantro and basil. Add the honey and lime juice. Stir to coat everything. Refrigerate for an hour or so. Drain off any excess water from the watermelon. Divide equally into the mini serving dishes. Serve and Enjoy !

INDEX

About the author.

ROBERT ZOLLWEG is a native of Toledo, Ohio and has been entertaining his friends and family for many years. Just Tasting Volume Two is all about serving a variety of wonderful appetizers, soups and salads in small mini portions at your next tasting party. Robert has worked in the tabletop industry for almost 40 years. He designs glassware, flatware and ceramic product for the retail and foodservice industry. He has worked with all of the major retailers from Crate and Barrel, Williams-Sonoma, Macy's, Pier One Imports, Cost Plus World Market, Bed Bath & Beyond, JCPenneys, Target, Walmart, Home Outfitters and Sears, to name a few. He has worked most of his professional career for Libbey Glass in Toledo, Ohio. He has traveled the world extensively looking for color and design trends and the right product to design and bring to the retail and foodservice marketplace. Robert is also an artist-painter and works primarily with acrylic on canvas using bold colors. His painting style has been called by many as abstract expressionism. He has always had a passion for entertaining, so Just Tasting Volume Two with more of these little mini appetizers, soups and salads recipes will continue this passion. He currently lives in his historic home in Toledo's Historic Old West End and in the artistic community of Saugatuck, Michigan.

To find out more information about Robert, visit his web site at:

www.zollwegart.com

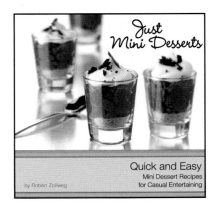

Just Mini Desserts

Quick and Easy
Mini Dessert Recipes
for Casual Entertaining
by Robert Zollweg

Just mini Cocktails

cocktails &
party drinks

Fun & Exciting Cocktail Recipes
for casual entertaining
and tasting parties
by Robert Zollweg

HOME decor
creative ideas with glass

Decorative Accessories
Wedding & Bridal
Holiday Centerpieces
Young & Modern
Craft Ideas
Bed & Bath

Fun & Exciting Home Décor
decorating ideas with
glass centerpieces
by Robert Zollweg

Just Tasting

mini appetizers
soups & salads

Quick and Easy Recipes
mini appetizers soups & salads
for casual entertaining
by Robert Zollweg

CRAFT BREWS
the right glass for the right beer

ales and lagers
beer cocktails
food pairing with craft beers
by Robert Zollweg

Just Baking
mini pies and casseroles

Quick and Easy
Single Serving Recipes
for casual family entertaining
by Robert Zollweg

COOL COCKTAILS
entertaining with cool glassware

cool cocktail recipes
entertaining with cocktails
non-alcoholic recipes
by Robert Zollweg

Just Mini Desserts
Volume 2

Quick and Easy Recipes
more mini dessert recipes
for casual entertaining
by Robert Zollweg

mini appetizers
soups & salads

Just Tasting
Volume 2

Quick and Easy Recipes
more mini appetizers soups & salads
for casual entertaining
by Robert Zollweg

If you have enjoyed this cookbook on mini appetizers, soups and salads, you may like my cookbook on mini desserts. The two compliment each other wonderfully. Both are about serving a variety of mini portions or tasters using various recipes that are simple and fun to do. If you would like more information about the Mini Dessert cookbook, go to: www.zollwegart .com